NATURE'S
CHILDREN

BALD EAGLES

by Emily J. Dolbear

Children's Press®

An Imprint of Scholastic Inc.
New York   Toronto   London   Auckland   Sydney
Mexico City   New Delhi   Hong Kong
Danbury, Connecticut

Content Consultant
Dr. Stephen S. Ditchkoff
Professor of Wildlife Sciences
Auburn University
Auburn, Alabama

Photographs © 2012: Alamy Images/Pete Ryan/National
Geographic Image Collection: 23; AP Images: 36 (Ben Margot),
39 (Leslie Baer/The Catalina Island Conservancy); Bob Italiano:
44 foreground, 45 foreground; Dreamstime: 2 background, 3
background, 44 background, 45 background (Jinyoung Lee), 27
(Naturediver), 28 (Neilneil), 1, 2 foreground, 3 foreground (Nemul),
4, 5 background, 20 (Richardseeley); Media Bakery: 40; National
Geographic: 5 top, 24 (Joel Sartore), 16, 19 (Klaus Nigge), 35
(Tom Murphy); Shutterstock, Inc.: 7 (Catcher of Light, Inc.), cover,
15, 43 (Colin Edwards Photography), 12 (Guido Vrola), 11 (Sandy
Hedgepeth), 32 (yykkaa); The Image Works: 5 bottom, 31 (Fritz
Polking), 8 (Hal Beral/V&W).

Library of Congress Cataloging-in-Publication Data
Dolbear, Emily J.
  Bald eagles/by Emily J. Dolbear.
      p. cm.—(Nature's children)
  Includes bibliographical references and index.
  ISBN-13: 978-0-531-20901-1 (lib. bdg.)
    ISBN-10: 0-531-20901-6 (lib. bdg.)
  ISBN-13: 978-0-531-21076-5 (pbk.)
    ISBN-10: 0-531-21076-6 (pbk.)
  1. Bald eagle—Juvenile literature. I. Title. II. Series.
  QL696.F32D65 2012
  598.9′42—dc23   2011031707

1 2 3 4 5 6 7 8 9 10 R 21 20 19 18 17 16 15 14 13 12

Bald Eagles

Class	Aves
Order	Falconiformes
Family	Accipitridae
Genus	*Haliaeetus*
Species	*Haliaeetus leucocephalus*
World distribution	North America
Habitat	Forested areas along rivers, lakes, marshes, and seacoasts
Distinctive physical characteristics	Dark brown body and wings; white head and tail; large, hooked yellow bill
Habits	Perches in trees overlooking water to search for food
Diet	Mainly eats fish; also known to eat birds, small mammals such as rabbits, and carrion

BALD EAGLES

Contents

CHAPTER 1

The Mighty Bald Eagle

The strength and beauty of the bald eagle have made it one of the most widely admired animals in North America. The bald eagle was officially selected as a national symbol for the United States of America in 1782. Many Native Americans consider the bird **sacred**.

An adult bald eagle is easy to recognize because of its white head and tail. The rest of its feathers are dark brown.

An adult bald eagle has several yellow body parts in addition to its striking dark and snow-white feathers. Its large **bill** is yellow. It also has yellow eyes and long, yellow feet. A bald eagle's feet end in curved claws called **talons**.

Bald eagles are not actually bald. Their heads are covered in white feathers. Bald eagles got their name from early settlers in North America. These settlers described them with a word similar to bald that meant "white."

The striking appearance of bald eagles makes them stand out from other large birds.

A Bird of Prey

Bald eagles are birds of **prey**, or **raptors**. This means that they hunt other animals for food. Other birds of prey include hawks, falcons, vultures, and owls.

Like nearly all birds of prey, bald eagles are most active during the day. They live in forested areas along rivers, lakes, marshes, and seacoasts. They perch in trees and look down into the water for fish to eat. They travel only as far as they need to find open water and fish to hunt. Bald eagles rarely **migrate** long distances as many other birds do. Some bald eagles even live in the same place all year.

FUN FACT! Bald eagles continue adding to their nests as the years go on. Sometimes they get so heavy that they break the tree's branches and fall down.

Bald eagles are effective hunters.

Big Birds

Bald eagles are large compared to most birds. A bald eagle's body can measure more than 3 feet (0.9 meters) tall. That is taller than a yardstick. Adult eagles weigh between 6 and 14 pounds (2.7 and 6.4 kilograms).

Male and female bald eagles look alike, whether they are young or fully grown. Female bald eagles are usually larger than the males. This is rare for most types of birds. But it is common among birds of prey.

The distance from tip to tip of a bald eagle's outstretched wings is impressive. Its **wingspan** can reach up to 7 feet (2.1 m). Its wings are almost completely flat in flight.

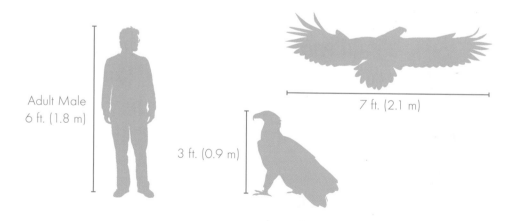

Adult Male
6 ft. (1.8 m)

3 ft. (0.9 m)

7 ft. (2.1 m)

It is sometimes difficult to tell male and female bald eagles apart.

CHAPTER 2

Tools for Survival

Adult bald eagles have few enemies in nature. To survive, they need a place to perch, a large body of open water nearby, and little contact with humans. Bald eagles in the wild can live to be more than 30 years old.

Bald eagles have many tools to help them survive. Those tools include their wings, eyes, talons, and bill. Each part of the bald eagle's body plays an important role in its survival.

FUN FACT! Eagles can carry about 4 pounds (1.8 kg) in their talons while flying.

Most eagles live near bodies of water where they can hunt for fish.

Wings and Eyes

The bald eagle has long, powerful wings. These wings help it glide on the wind. Rising currents of warm air called **thermals** also provide lift in flight. The bald eagle saves its energy by gliding instead of flapping its wings.

Bald eagles swoop down suddenly to catch their meals. They can fly as fast as 60 miles (97 kilometers) an hour. They can move even faster in a dive. But how do they know when to dive down?

Sometimes people who notice details are described as having an "eagle eye." This is because eagles have excellent eyesight. A bald eagle's eyesight is at least four times better than a human's. Bald eagles can see ahead and to the side of them at the same time. Their large eyes allow them to spot prey from more than 1 mile (1.6 km) away.

Bald eagles pay close attention to the ground, looking for food, as they glide through the air.

Sharp Talons

A flying bald eagle spots a fish swimming in the lake below. The eagle dives from the sky and thrusts out its large feet near the water's surface to seize its prey. Then it relies on its talons to catch the fish.

All eagles have four toes on each foot. There are three toes at the front of the foot and one in the back. Tiny spikes underneath the toes help the eagle hold a fish that may be slippery. Each toe has a piercing talon at its tip. A talon can measure 1.5 inches (3.8 centimeters) long.

The bald eagle plucks the fish from the water with its sharp talons. If the fish is still alive, the talons will soon crush and kill it. A bald eagle can use its talons to carry a catch that is about half its own weight.

Eagles dive down, grab a fish, and return to the sky in one smooth motion.

A Useful Bill

The bald eagle flies to a nearby tree with its catch. It is safer there. Now the eagle uses yet another body part to feed itself. It tears and eats pieces of the fish with its very useful hooked bill. Eagles sometimes wade into shallow water and use their bills to snatch fish.

Bald eagles also feed on waterbirds such as ducks, gulls, and Canada geese. Squirrels, raccoons, prairie dogs, and even foxes are other food sources. Hunting these animals usually requires more work than hunting fish. Bald eagles will steal food from other birds of prey if they get the chance.

Dead animal flesh called **carrion** feeds a hungry bald eagle. A bald eagle might find an animal killed on the highway or a seal washed up on the seashore. No matter what it is eating, a bald eagle uses its hooked bill to help get every last bit of food.

Eagles can tear at even the toughest meats with their strong bills.

CHAPTER 3

A Family Affair

Bald eagles probably **mate** for life once they are paired together. Bald eagles usually lay their eggs in large nests at the tops of trees. They occasionally place their nests on cliffs. Eagle nests are called **aeries**.

A bald eagle pair builds its nest together. The eagles search for and carry branches, sticks, and twigs to construct the aerie. Then they line it with grasses, moss, and soft feathers to protect and warm the fragile eggs. It can take months to complete an aerie. A bald eagle pair often uses the same aerie year after year.

Bald eagles build the biggest bird nests in the world. One of the largest bald eagle nests was recorded in St. Petersburg, Florida. It was more than 9 feet (2.7 m) across and 20 feet (6 m) deep. It was estimated to weigh more than 4,000 pounds (1,814 kg). Most cars don't weight that much!

An average bald eagle nest is about 4 to 6 feet (1.2 to 1.8 m) wide.

Eggs in the Nest

The female bald eagle lays her first egg between 5 and 10 days after mating. The dull white egg measures about 3 inches (7.6 cm) long. Each **clutch** usually has two eggs. Sometimes it contains one or three eggs.

The female sits on the eggs to warm them so that they will hatch. It takes about five weeks. The male helps **incubate** the eggs. He also hunts to feed the pair and maintains the nest.

Bald eagle eggs are laid a few days apart. They also hatch a few days apart. This allows the first **eaglet** to eat without competition. Younger eaglets are not as likely to survive as their older siblings. They often get less to eat.

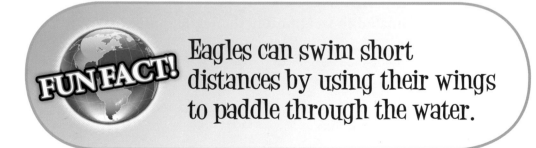

FUN FACT! Eagles can swim short distances by using their wings to paddle through the water.

Eagle parents guard their eggs and eaglets carefully.

New Eaglets

It can take more than a day for an eaglet to fully hatch out of its egg. An eaglet is weak and helpless after hatching. A new eaglet weighs only about 3 ounces (85 grams). It is born with its eyes open. Soft, gray feathers cover its tiny body.

Both parents help raise their new eaglets. They bring food to the nest. The eaglets grow quickly. Their parents protect them from danger. There is always a risk that a hungry crow, owl, or snake might snatch an eaglet from the nest.

Eaglets begin growing feathers after about a month. They are able to feed themselves soon after that. They grow the feathers they need to fly when they are about three months old. Then they are ready for flight.

Young eagles face many challenges after hatching. They can starve. They can fall out of the nest. They can crash the first time they try to fly. It is not surprising that most eagles do not survive their first year.

Baby eagles do not look like their parents when they are born.

Juvenile Eagles

A **juvenile** eagle is an eagle that is not fully grown. Juvenile eagles can fly. But they do not yet look like adults. A juvenile eagle has a mixture of dark brown and white feathers. Its bill is dark brown at first, but it slowly turns yellow as the eagle grows.

Bald eagles do not look like their parents until they are four or five years old. By that age, a bald eagle has grown its adult feathers, or **plumage**. Its head and tail are now white. It has learned how to fly and hunt for its own food. The bald eagle is now able to find a mate, build a nest, and raise its own young.

FUN FACT! Founding Father Benjamin Franklin believed that the wild turkey would make a better national symbol than the bald eagle.

Juveniles fly and hunt for food just as their parents do.

CHAPTER 4

Sea Eagles and Other Relatives

Bald eagles are part of a **genus** of birds called *Haliaeetus* (hah-lee-ay-EET-us). That means "sea eagle" in Latin. All the birds in this group feed mainly on fish.

Sea eagles live near large bodies of water. They are found in all parts of the world except South America. These birds have large bills. Their lower legs have no feathers. Their toes are rough underneath to help them grip slippery fish.

FUN FACT! If a bald eagle loses a feather on one wing, it will also shed a feather from the other wing so that it stays balanced.

Most bald eagles live near the many lakes and rivers of North America.

The Closest Relative

The bald eagle is the only sea eagle **species** found in North America. Where do the other sea eagles live? What does the bald eagle's closest relative look like?

The white-tailed sea eagle is the bald eagle's closest relative. It is found far from North America. The white-tailed sea eagle lives in Europe and Asia. It looks like a bald eagle except it has a tan head. The two relatives are similar in appearance. But they cannot **breed** together.

The African fish eagle is sometimes called the bald eagle's twin. The two species live far away from each other, but they look almost exactly alike. Like bald eagles, African fish eagles have white heads and brown bodies. They swoop down toward water to snatch fish with their long talons.

The white-tailed sea eagle is the largest bird of prey in the United Kingdom.

Not a Sea Eagle at All

Golden eagles live alongside bald eagles in many parts of North America. But golden eagles are not sea eagles. They belong to a different genus. These eagles are also found in Asia, northern Africa, and Europe.

Some bird-watchers mistake juvenile bald eagles for golden eagles. But golden eagles are not very closely related to bald eagles. Golden eagle bodies have brown feathers. On the head and neck are light golden feathers. Unlike an adult bald eagle, a golden eagle has dark eyes and a gray bill. It also has feathered legs.

Golden eagles feed on hares, squirrels, mice, and sometimes birds. They rarely eat fish. Golden eagles are some of North America's largest birds of prey.

The golden eagle is Mexico's national bird.

CHAPTER 5

A Wildlife Story

More than half a million bald eagles soared the skies of North America in the 1600s. But when European settlers arrived, they began shooting these birds of prey. They believed the eagles were killing their farm animals. Alaska even paid its residents to hunt bald eagles during the early 1900s.

Americans realized by the 1930s that the bald eagle was disappearing. The U.S. government passed the Bald and Golden Eagle Protection Act in 1940. This law made it illegal to kill, hurt, or disturb these eagles. It also protected their nests and eggs.

No matter how close they come to humans, bald eagles remain protected by law.

New Threats

Even under the Protection Act of 1940, by 1963 fewer than 500 bald eagle pairs were nesting in the United States, not including Alaska. Bald eagles were facing **extinction**. They were on track to die out completely in most of North America.

What was causing the bald eagle numbers to drop? Hunting and loss of natural lands were two major reasons. A powerful chemical called DDT was another problem. Farmers began spraying their crops with DDT in the 1940s. This **pesticide** killed insects that were harmful to plants and people. But the chemical also damaged wildlife such as bald eagles.

Many bald eagles ate fish that had absorbed the pesticide from lakes and rivers. Affected eagles began producing eggs with thin shells. Fragile eggs cracked before the eaglets were ready to hatch. This resulted in fewer eagles being born.

Scientists rescued and cared for many fragile eggs that had been affected by DDT until they were ready to hatch.

Recovery

The dangers of DDT led to its ban in the United States and Canada in 1972. The U.S. government passed the **Endangered** Species Act the next year. This law included protection for bald eagles. It also spurred scientists and others into action. They relocated wild eaglets from Alaska to other parts of the United States. They helped bald eagles in captivity to breed. They kept a close eye on nests, eggs, and bald eagles in the wild. The eagle count increased faster than anyone expected.

This wildlife story ends with success. By 1995, the U.S. Fish and Wildlife Service no longer considered the bald eagle endangered. But the bird was still listed as a **threatened** species in the lower 48 U.S. states, which doesn't include Alaska and Hawaii.

Scientists raised captive baby eagles before returning them to the wild.

The Future

In 2007, the bald eagle was removed entirely from the federal list of threatened and endangered species. The Bald and Golden Eagle Protection Act of 1940 continues to outlaw the harming of a bald eagle.

Today, there are nearly 10,000 breeding pairs in the lower 48 states. The total population in North America is more than 100,000 bald eagles. More than half of them live in Alaska and Canada.

Government agencies need to monitor birds in the wild for this success story to continue. Preserving the lands where bald eagles live and breed will keep their numbers growing.

FUN FACT! If an eagle's stomach is full, it can store extra food in a throat pouch called a crop and digest the food at a later time.

Scientists continue to learn more about bald eagles.

Words to Know

aeries (AIR-ees) — eagle nests

bill (BIL) — the beak or jaws of a bird

breed (BREED) — to mate and give birth to young

carrion (KAR-ee-uhn) — dead animal flesh

clutch (KLUHCH) — a nest of eggs

eaglet (EE-glit) — a young eagle

endangered (en-DAYN-jurd) — at risk of becoming extinct, usually because of human activity

extinction (ik-STINGKT-shuhn) —complete disappearance of a species from a certain area or from the entire world

genus (JEE-nuhs) — a group of related plants or animals that is larger than a species but smaller than a family

incubate (ING-kyuh-bate) — to keep eggs warm before they hatch

juvenile (JOO-vuh-nuhl) — not fully grown

mate (MAYT) — to join together to produce babies

migrate (MY-grayt) — to move from one area to another

pesticide (PES-ti-side) — a chemical used to kill pests, such as insects

plumage (PLOO-mij) — a bird's feathers, considered as a whole prey (PRAY) — an animal that's hunted by another animal for food

raptors (RAP-turz) — birds of prey, such as eagles, hawks, falcons, vultures, and owls

sacred (SAY-krid) — very important and deserving great respect

species (SPEE-sheez) — one of the groups into which animals and plants of the same genus are divided

talons (TAL-uhns) — sharp claws of a bird

thermals (THUR-muhls) — rising currents of warm air

threatened (THRET-uhnd) — at risk of becoming endangered

wingspan (WING-span) — the distance from the end of one wing to the end of the other wing on a bird

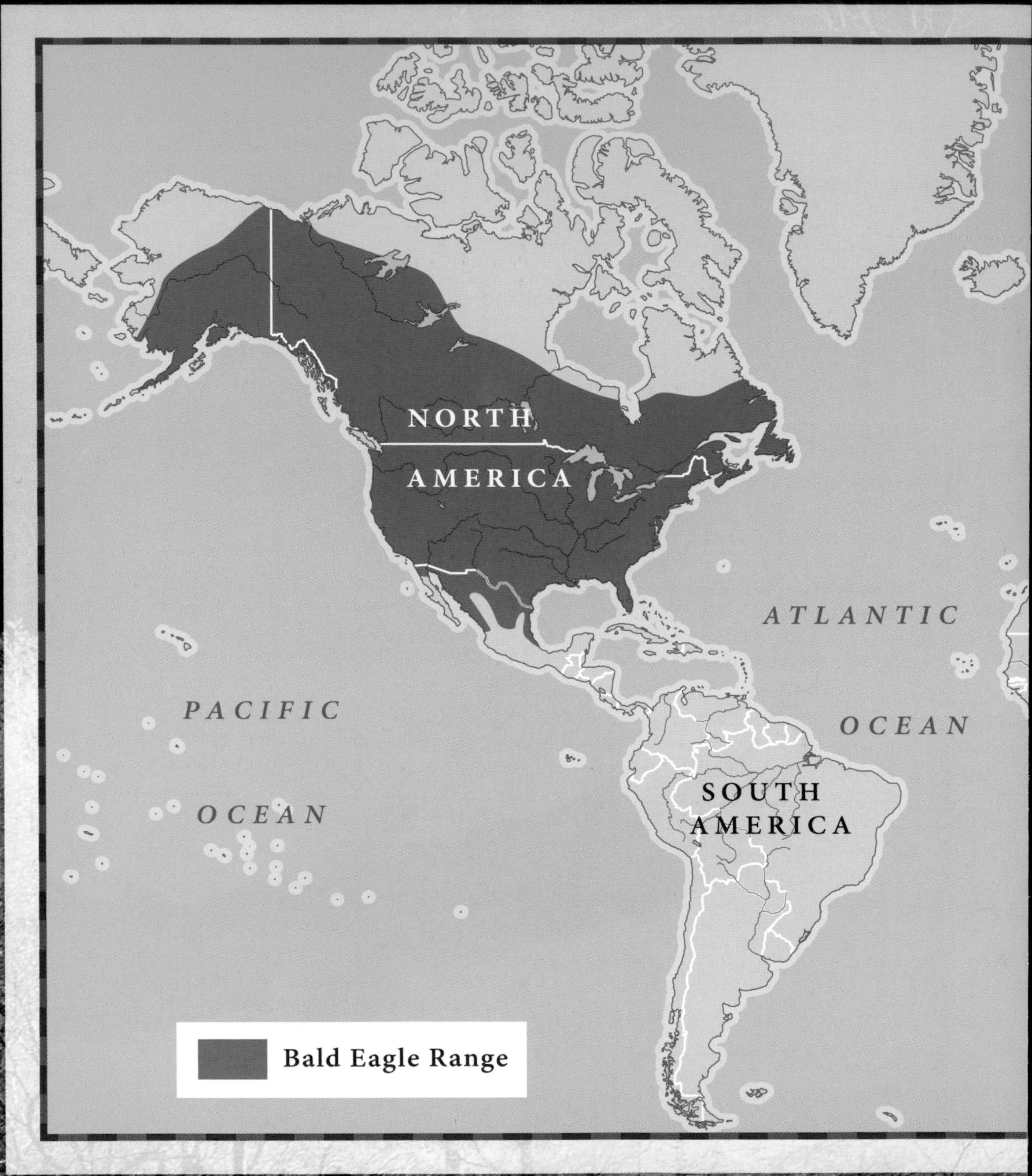

NORTH AMERICA

ATLANTIC

PACIFIC

OCEAN

OCEAN

SOUTH AMERICA

Bald Eagle Range

ARCTIC OCEAN

EUROPE

ASIA

AFRICA

PACIFIC OCEAN

INDIAN OCEAN

AUSTRALIA

Find Out More

Books

Gray, Susan H. *Bald Eagle*. Ann Arbor, MI: Cherry Lake Publishing, 2009.

Raven, Margot Theis. *Challenger: America's Favorite Eagle*. Chelsea, MI: Sleeping Bear Press, 2005.

Wilcox, Charlotte. *Bald Eagles*. Minneapolis: Carolrhoda Books, 2003.

Web Sites

Defenders of Wildlife—Bald Eagle
www.defenders.org/wildlife_and_habitat/wildlife/bald_eagle.php
Get facts and keep up with the latest information about threats to the bald eagle.

National Geographic Kids—Bald Eagle
http://kids.nationalgeographic.com/kids/animals/creaturefeature/baldeagle
Check out this site for bald eagle facts and photos. You can also listen to a sound clip of a bald eagle and watch a short video of a mother tending to her young.

Visit this Scholastic web site for more information on bald eagles:
www.factsfornow.scholastic.com

Index

About the Author

A graduate of Williams College, Emily J. Dolbear has worked as a nonfiction editor and author for more than 15 years. She lives with her family in Brookline, Massachusetts. Her state is home to more than 100 wintering bald eagles.